BASIC RESPECT

BASIC RESPECT
My Gift to the World

BY TERI BOLDEN

Teri C Bolden Publishing

©2017 Teri Bolden. All Rights Reserved under United States and International Copyright Laws. This book, including contents and/or cover, may not be reproduced in whole or part in any form without the written consent of the author and/or publisher.

ISBN 978-0-692-79078-6

Printed in the United States of America

Definitions are taken from the Merriam-Webster dictionary and the Macmillan dictionary.

For more information or to order copies, contact Teri Bolden via email at Dreamnr2@outlook.com.

I dedicate this book to my mom and dad, Mr. Arthur D. and the late Lucy Mae Cotman. My mom was a woman of supreme virtue. She had morals, values, and principles that made her stand out as a woman with pure class. I am so thankful for the examples she set. I would like to thank my dad for always being there and providing me with love, stability, and guidance throughout the years.

Acknowledgments

I would like to acknowledge and thank Ms. Pamela Wakefield for listening to me in 2011 when I said I wanted to write a book. She heard me, encouraged me, and inspired me to finally get it done. Pamela kept telling me there was a book inside of me, and with her believing in me, and my believing in myself, it has become a reality. See what happens when you believe.

I would also like to acknowledge my husband, Johnny, my daughter, Andrea, and siblings Lindoria, Arthur, and Janel for always being there with endless support.

Table of Contents

Introduction

Chapter 1 Respect Starts at Home

Chapter 2 Respecting and Loving Yourself

Chapter 3 Watch Your Tone

Chapter 4 Attitude: It's Not All About You!

Chapter 5 Family, Marriage, Friendships

Chapter 6 Respect One Woman to Another

Chapter 7 Respect Yourself and Others Will Follow

What Respect Means to Others

About the Author

Introduction

I was led to write this book by simply seeing the need for people to start respecting themselves and respecting others. I believe many incidents and situations could be avoided if things were handled in a respectful manner.

Too often we point the finger at everyone else but fail to look within. If the truth be told we all are works in progress, trying to improve ourselves, as we continually learn ourselves. My hope is that when people read my book they will be enlightened, uplifted, and inspired and that it will bring change to those who are willing to take the first step to make a difference.

My desire is that after everyone reads this book they will strive to be the best they can be by respecting themselves and others, which can promote better lives for our families and communities. Respect, even in small doses, can go a long way. Change can start with you! Let me show you how.

Read on . . .

Mom & Dad

Chapter 1

Respect Starts at Home

My mom and dad instilled in me and my siblings at a very young age the beauty and importance of respect. They made sure it was displayed on a regular basis. From as far as I can remember, there has always been the expectation of learning and practicing some basic type of respect in, as well as out of, our home. It is a practice that we carried into our adult lives. Unfortunately, this may not have been the case in everyone's home. Therefore, in order for us to discuss respect and how it begins, we have to examine what children are being taught at home.

Children learn best by examples: by what they see, what they've been exposed to, or what they've experienced. That's why it's important that as parents we are good role models and recognize our children as the "sponges" they are by making sure that what they absorb are things that are good and kind and display love.

And if we find ourselves having to go back and brush up on respect skills, than it's no better time than the present to start.

In order for us to get a better understanding of respect, let's define respect.

Respect is defined as a feeling of admiring someone or something that is good, valuable, important, . . . and to show honor or esteem and high regard for (Merriam-Webster dictionary).

The Macmillan dictionary also defines respect *as a feeling of admiration that you have for someone because of their personal qualities, their achievements, or their status and that you treat them in a polite and kind way.*

As parents, if we lay out the foundation by displaying respect in our homes, our children will learn respectful behavior that will teach them how to respect people in and out of their homes, communities, parents, elders, people in authority, and so forth. Therefore, in order for change to occur with our children and teenagers, it must first start with us, the parents.

Chapter 2

Respecting and Loving Yourself

There are things that we learn as children that stay with us our entire lives. Two important lessons should be self-love and self-respect. What is self-love? Self-love is the belief that you are a valuable and worthy person. An example of self-love is when you have a positive view of yourself and are confident of yourself and your place in the world. Self-love is loving oneself in a way that is not arrogant or conceited but caring about oneself and taking responsibility.

Another lesson is self-respect. Self-respect is defined as holding yourself in high esteem and believing that you are a good person worthy of being treated well. Self-respect is pride and confidence in oneself; a feeling that one is behaving with honor and dignity. An example of self-respect is when you know you deserve to be treated right, and as a result, you do not tolerate certain behavior from others or allow someone to mistreat you.

It is very important that you start with at least these two foundational principles, self-love and self-respect, to build on. It can be the foundation for having a stable home, life, and relationships that are built on love and respect.

Let's face it. Sometimes we give respect to others, and sometimes we don't. Only we know why we do the things we do when it comes to respecting others. Is it that we feel the person we are dealing with doesn't deserve our respect, or is it that we don't know how to display or give respect?

If we are honest with ourselves, we might even see there are many races and cultures that can benefit from learning how to respect each other's diversity. You can have respect without love, but you can't have true love without R-E-S-P-E-C-T.

All of us can learn a lesson or two about respect, especially among our youth. Ask yourself a serious question: Did I get the basic principles of respect as a child? And were they

Respecting and Loving Yourself

displayed in words, lessons taught, actions and examples set? I think it would be safe to say some of us may have missed the bus of respect. My wish is that this book will inspire people to give respect, as well as demand it, and provide a smoother and more fulfilling ride through your life, today, tomorrow, and always.

Let's talk about that four-letter word L-O-V-E. Love is defined as a strong affection or liking for someone or something. A passionate affection of one person for another. People use the word *love* all the time, with little or no thought of what it really means. There are actions and consequences associated with love. If you want love or promise to give love, you better know what it entails.

When you do the work of working on yourself, you can begin to truly love and respect others. Sometimes we love ourselves, but not enough in certain areas. One area of self-love that is not being displayed enough and can manifest itself is in relationships. If someone is toxic to your well-being or is not loving and respecting you in a way you deserve to be treated, then it's time to talk.

Once you talk and communicate about your concerns to the other person and things don't change or get better, and you stay in the relationship anyway, that's when self-love is not enough or strong enough! People live this way every day. The best time to exercise self-love is before you marry someone. However, if you are in a relationship and if things don't change or get better, remember to continue exercising self-love. Working on self is a process; the more you progress with improving self, the more consideration you may have for others. Consideration is the act of considering, and to have thoughtful regard for others and their feelings. Your thoughts can become your actions, and your actions are the results of your thoughts, which lead to your behavior. Enough said.

Chapter 3

Watch Your Tone

The tone we use, and how we speak and address one another is so important. The tone or manner in which we say things makes all the difference in how we affect others. Tone is defined as a quality, feeling, or attitude expressed by the words that are used when someone speaks or writes. We adopt a variety of tones in our day-to-day speech, and the pitch of our speech determines what message we desire to convey to the other person.

For example, if you were my customer, and I told you "go over there, have a seat, and I'll be right with you," then that should be fine with you. But imagine my saying that in a loud, frustrated voice, in a harsh tone, and

Basic Respect

with sarcasm. How would that make you feel? The tone and manner in which I said it makes all the difference in how I made you feel and how you feel about me. If you want to be heard, as well as respected, it would be beneficial to watch your tone!

I know there are times when being heard and demanding respect can mean getting loud and being direct. But there is a time and place for everything. If you take the time to think about what you say and how you say it, your tone may not change, but at least you won't regret having said it.

Generally if we try using a respectful tone, most of the times things won't escalate because of frustration. If we all would watch our tone and communicate in a respectful manner, things could change for the better.

It's also important to show respect in how we address others. For some reason, girls of a particular age find it appropriate to call women of a certain age "sweetie." In my opinion, *sweetie* is not always appropriate, especially when you are half their age, and they are not someone you personally know. Now I realize this can be a term of endearment, but only use it when it's appropriate, and not when it could possibly be offensive to someone else.

Watch Your Tone

Then there are ways when speaking to our children requires certain words and tones as well. We should still be mindful that children can be very sensitive and should be addressed with a warm and loving tone. This tone teaches children a sense of love, but also one of respect!

Chapter 4

Attitude: It's Not All About You!

For some reason or another, some people seem to think it's ALWAYS about them. Why do you think that is? My experiences have been that people think it should be all about them, because a lot of us, whether we want to admit it or not, are selfish! Yes, I said it, selfish! We get so absorbed in what we're doing that we don't realize our behavior and its effect on others. In other words, when we do something for self and don't take the time to consider and/or think about how it may affect other people, it is selfishness. In the moment we simply are doing what makes US happy.

Attitude: It's Not All About You!

For example, let's take a look at our babies. The behaviors of babies and young children are often innate, meaning they are born this way. This is when parenting and teaching should guide the child's behavior in a positive direction. We generally teach what we know and what we believe. No matter what we do, respect and self-love should always be in those teachings. The key is having balance of respect and self-love. Unfortunately, finding that balance can sometimes be a problem. I will forever be grateful to my parents for instilling in me a good understanding of how to be treated and how to treat others.

Our childhood is the foundation for everything. It shapes our future into being the adults we will become. Parents should do their best to provide a wonderful, loving, nurturing, and caring environment for their children. Love and respect are the two things that money can't buy. You may be able to get superficial love, love with conditions, but it's nothing like

Basic Respect

the real thing. Life experiences have shown us that people need people. It should never be just about you, even if we think it should be. In order to be part of a successful and winning team, and add more value to your life, start with this piece of advice: Give respect to receive R-E-S-P-E-C-T! I once heard, sometimes in life it's your attitude, not your aptitude that will help you reach your altitude.

Chapter 5

Family, Marriage, and Friendships

Let's face it, there are many challenges when it comes to families, marriages, and friendships! I believe if we are more patient in our relationships and honor them with the love and respect they deserve, they could flourish and thrive. Unfortunately, more often than not, that's not the case. A lot depends on what these relationships may mean to you that determines the energy you give to them and how much work you are willing to put into maintaining and keeping them.

Sometimes these relationships can be one-sided. All people involved in the relationship need to give positive energy and take the responsibility to help the relationship grow, stay alive, and be healthy. If not, these relationships will not flourish but will wither and sometimes are gone forever.

If you treasure and value a particular relationship, then you must be willing to put in the work to keep it functional and healthy. Often times when relationships don't work out for one reason or another, everyone seem to think they aren't part of the problem, and the other person is blamed. This is not always the truth.

You must put in the work in order for relationships to survive. So if you are not part of the solution, you could very well be part of the problem. People don't like to admit they could be part of the problem, and this is how relationships start to die. Especially when neither party is giving the relationship what it may need at that time to move in the direction of growth. We simply stop nourishing it and then wonder what happened. So when you feel that any relationship is changing, but not for the better, start talking about what you feel immediately.

Chapter 6

Respect One Woman to Another

Some women are in need of improvement when it comes to respecting each other, especially in relationships that involve men. Whether it is a friend, boyfriend, or spouse, the relationship between two women is not always one of mutual respect. I realize people come from different walks of life and may see the same situation from different perspectives.

There are times when a woman knows that a man is in a relationship and insists on being disrespectful to the other woman. It's truly not what you do, but how you do it, that makes the difference in being respectful or disrespectful.

Basic Respect

Having respect for yourself is having respect for another woman. If your issue is with the man, conduct yourself in a manner that respects yourself, the man, and even the other woman. Start by giving women, and especially those who have not done anything to you, some basic respect. Women can play many games when it comes to relationships pertaining to men. Trust me when I say, we know what we are doing when we decide to be disrespectful to another woman. This type of behavior does a disservice to all women and weakens unity. Let's just say, *check yourself before you wreck yourself!*

Even if he deserves what he has coming to him, which could mean losing both women, as well as experiencing their wrath, it's not worth your dignity or self-respect to waste time being disrespectful. In relationships, there are many elements and dynamics that may not always present themselves! Oftentimes you can't control what someone else does; you can only control what you do. As women, we all deserve from one another and should give each other respect. You don't have forever to do what you know hopefully in your heart is the right thing, so why not start today by being the change you want to see!

Chapter 7

Respect Yourself and Others Will Follow

I hope we as a people decide to really take the time to work on how we treat one another. I know we are not perfect, but start by asking yourself when you had to deal with a situation, "Was that the best or most respectful way to handle that situation or confront someone?" Also, when it comes to allowing someone to treat you a certain way, make sure it's done with respect.

The word *respect* is used and wanted by many, but the action of the word often times is not given. People constantly say that they were disrespected, someone was disrespectful, or they had no respect for a situation. When an incidence of respect occurs and you are involved, if you are not part of a solution, you ARE part of the problem. It starts with the adults practicing what they are preaching to the children.

How can you expect our children of the future to get or learn something that we haven't taken time to learn and practice ourselves on a daily basis? There is always room for improvement in this area. If you want people to do their best, you have to give your best. If you want people to respect you and the law, you have to respect them and the law. If you want the world to be a better place, then let it start with you becoming a better you. Young, old, rich or poor, man, boy, woman, or girl, everyone deserves it! Have some . . . RESPECT by respecting yourself and others!

What Respect Means to Others

I asked twelve individuals ranging from twenty-five to eighty years old to define what respect means to them. Here are their responses.

****

C.D., *female, age 29, states respect means the appreciation for someone's character.*

B.A., *female, age 63, states respect means to honor and to admire.*

C.A., *male, age 80, states respect means something you have to give in order to receive.*

B.T., *female, age 27, states respect means to honor and to have reverence for someone.*

Basic Respect

H.A., female, age 39, states respect means taking others' feelings into consideration.

R.W., female, age 25, states respect means freedom.

B.J., male, age 51, states respect means a mirror image of how you want to be treated.

I.T., female, age 25, states respect means to acknowledge.

S.M., female, age 70, states respect means to treat someone the way you want to be treated.

R.B., female, age 54, states respect means to not have a sense of entitlement.

H.I., male, age 52, states respect is looking up to a person, keeping them in mind before you make decisions, thinking about the person's feelings, and listening to their thoughts. Respect also means to value!!!

W.B., female, age 51, states self-respect is a feeling of pride, it's being proud of who you are, how you look, and how you present yourself to the public. You have to be honest and always keep it 100%. In short, self-respect is loving who you are and being proud enough to take a stand if necessary. Some people can't handle a person

What does Respect Mean to You?

who is overconfident. But the right mixture of confidence and self-respect, most people will appreciate. Those who are insecure about themselves usually look for people to follow. They search for people to imitate, and they are followers. They usually have little self-respect.

What does Respect Mean to You?

_____
_____
_____
_____
_____
_____
_____
_____
_____
_____
_____
_____
_____
_____
_____
_____
_____
_____

What does Respect Mean to You?

About the Author

Teri Bolden is a wife, mother, sister, and loyal friend. She is passionate about wanting people to treat each other with respect. She has learned that respect is at the top of the list of what everyone wants and deserves! Starting

About the Author

back to the time when Teri was a little girl, treating people with respect has always been important to her.

As an entrepreneur, she has been able to practice how to treat the general public and has learned some things about respecting others along the way. One of her mottos is to *treat people the way you want to be treated, and don't expect something from someone that you are not willing to give.*

Teri resides in Virginia and enjoys spending time with her family and friends, exercising, singing, reading, going to the movies, eating out, and riding her bike.

To contact Teri, or to purchase her book, email her at dreamnr2@outlook.com.

www.ingramcontent.com/pod-product-compliance
Lightning Source LLC
Chambersburg PA
CBHW071109010526
44110CB00059B/1929